Harmonic Minor, Melodic M' nd Diminished Scales for (

for all styles, with theory, modal applications and typical chord progressions

by Barrett Tagliarino

To Download Audio, Go To:

monsterguitars.com/hmd

The password is "alter"

You will download a zip file of 74 mp3s. When the book refers to a track number, use the filename with the same number on your listening device. The click track is slightly panned to the left channel, so you can adjust its relative volume somewhat by using your balance control. On examples that include chords, they are panned slightly to the right.

About the Author

Barrett Tagliarino is a Los Angeles-based solo artist, session guitarist, vocalist, and instructor. Since 1989 he has been a full-time faculty member at Musicians Institute, where he teaches core and elective classes in improvisation styles, technique, reading, ear training, and theory. His previous books include *Interval Studies and Lead Guitar Technique*, *Rhythmic Lead Guitar*, the *Guitar Reading Workbook*, *Chord Tone Soloing*, and the *Guitar Fretboard Workbook*. Barrett's two solo CDs, *Moe's Art* and *Throttle Twister*, showcase his unique approach to composition and life-long addiction to the guitar.

For Barrett's latest instructional materials, recordings, videos, blog posts, performance dates, etc., please visit his website, monsterguitars.com.

Barrett Tagliarino uses and endorses Suhr guitars, Kaliphoria amplifiers, D'Addario strings, and Planet Waves accessories.

ISBN-13
978-0-9802353-5-7

ISBN-10
0-9802353-5-9

Copyright © 2012 Behemoth Publishers
All rights reserved.

Except as permitted under the United States Copyright Act of 1976, no part of this publication may be reproduced or distributed in any form without prior written permission of the publisher.

Contents

Introduction

When soloing over chord progressions you can often encounter colorful chords that temporarily clash with the normal scale that corresponds to the key center. Knowledge of harmonic minor, melodic minor, and diminished scales—and their modes—lets you improvise over these non-diatonic chords with creative freedom, and will also help you bring more variety into your own compositions.

We'll learn positional patterns for these three scales to cover the fretboard. Interval studies will be used to reinforce these scale shapes and connect the fingering moves to your ears. We'll practice applying the scales in various modal contexts, and learn a few useful licks that show how they can create interest when properly applied in solos and melodies.

Prerequisites

Because of the subject matter this book assumes some prior experience on your part, and it moves at a slightly faster pace than my others.

A basic knowledge of the correct spelling of intervals, chords, and scales is assumed, as well as basic theoretical terms like *diatonic* and *enharmonic* (e.g., C♭ = B). You should also know names of the notes on the fretboard and the CAGED-based five-pattern fretboard system (*Guitar Fretboard Workbook*).

Because the scales in this book require focused application over fleeting non-diatonic chords, a rudimentary grasp of counting bars, beats, and beat divisions will also be helpful (*Rhythmic Lead Guitar*, *Guitar Reading Workbook*). Playing a distinctive tone from one of these scales as little as an eighth note early or late can make your soloing sound worse instead of better.

The book will be easier if you come to it already knowing the modes of the major scale, and are able to apply them to major and minor keys and modal chord progressions (*Interval Studies and Lead Guitar Technique*). It will also help if you have worked on following chord changes with at least single target tones, and to some extent, triads and 7th arpeggios (*Chord Tone Soloing*).

Finally, you should also know how to create a practice schedule, stick to it, and update it at a pace that is appropriate for you. Good practice habits are essential to your progress; they're discussed at length in *Chord Tone Soloing* and in *Interval Studies and Lead Guitar Technique*.

The Work

It's not enough to play through the book's examples once or twice and move on. In order to really learn to apply the new scales, especially when improvising, you'll have to practice the patterns in multiple keys until they're solidly in long-term memory. The interval studies shown are only a small sample of the useful possibilities. Practice all the scale patterns in interval studies from 3rds through 7ths, and then longer sequences like the 1-3-4-2 sawtooth example in Unit 3. Full matrices of intervallic permutations are explained in *Interval Studies and Lead Guitar Technique*.

Any licks or melodic examples in the book are non-essential, though they do represent distillations of the desired sounds for each mode, with most of the relevant notes "correctly" (for want of a better word) placed on or off the beat. Whether you like these enough to let them influence your vocabulary or not is up to you. Either way, you'll still probably want to come up with some of your own.

Some of the material in this book might sound a bit strange to you at first. These sounds are often inserted into popular music in ways that go unnoticed by the untrained ear. With time and practice you will learn to recognize these scales and and their accompanying chords in places you might not have expected, and you'll start to understand how they work.

Finally, while some music is meant for mass consumption and should be easy for anyone to follow, there is also the kind that requires more attention from and involvement of the listener. Both have their place, and part of your job as a professional is to decide what is appropriate for the situation.

Unit 1: Harmonic Minor

We can create a harmonic minor scale pattern by raising the 7th degree of a natural minor scale. This creates an augmented 2nd between steps 6 and 7. Five patterns in D minor are shown.

Harmonic Minor Scale

1	M2	m3	P4	P5	m6	M7	P8

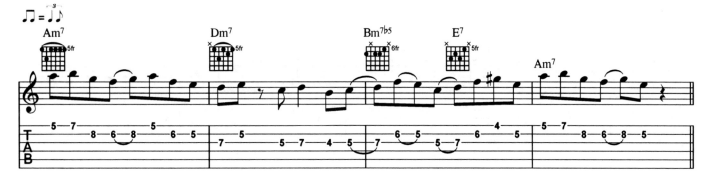

Pattern 1 Pattern 2 Pattern 3 Pattern 4 Pattern 5

The augmented 2nds may be played across two strings (e.g., Pattern 1) or as a stretch (Pattern 3). Moving the 7th changes your options for hammer-ons and pulloffs.

> Practice harmonic minor scales in different keys. If you already know natural minor scale patterns, remember that these are the same but with a raised seventh degree. If necessary, work with just one pattern, adding the others over the course of several weeks.

The fingerings above are in the key of D minor to fit the entire five-pattern scheme on the fretboard in order. The following examples, however, start with Pattern 4 of A harmonic minor at the 5th fret.

The major 7th (also called the *leading tone*) in this minor scale and its accompanying chords (most often V, V7, viidim, or viidim7) increase the tension and resolution to the i minor chord. The leading tone is melodically strong only during one of these chords and is either avoided or used as a special tone (e.g., passing between two strong tones) over the other chords in the minor key. It's therefore important to work on getting in and out of the scale quickly, returning to natural minor. Here harmonic is found over the E7 only. The A Aeolian or natural minor scale is played over the i, iv, and ii chords.

Track 1

Here some diatonic 3rd intervals in a sawtooth pattern are incorporated into an exercise that moves from A natural minor to A harmonic minor and back again.

Track 2

Playing harmonic minor directly over a im or im7 chord can be tricky. First try it over any chord in the minor key **except** i, ♭III, or ♭VII (Am, C, or G in this key). It especially fits V and vii (E or G♯dim).

To use harmonic minor over all the chords in a minor progression requires some care because of its inherent tension and resolution. To keep a line from resolving prematurely, arrange for any A played during E7 to fall on an upbeat. When/as the chord resolves, the root of the scale can be on the beat. The leading tone can be used over the Am, but try to keep it on the upbeats at first. Simply put, place chord tones on the beat while you're learning to follow the changes.

Track 3

Here's another short study, this time exploring diatonic 4th intervals. Because the 7th degree in measure 4 falls on the upbeat, depending on the accompaniment a raised 7th should work.

Track 4

This 16-bar rock solo uses the G harmonic minor scale almost exclusively. The simple 8-bar progression starts at measure 2, after a long pickup phrase. In measures 3, 11, and 16 there are connected bends, releases, and hammer-ons. Only pick the first of the three notes in these licks (for example starting at beat 2 of measure 3, marked with an asterisk). In measure 17 there is an artificial harmonic played with the pick and side of the thumb exactly half the distance between the fretted note and the bridge.

Track 5

Scale Harmony

Harmonizing the harmonic minor scale produces new chords for degrees i, III, V, and vii in a minor key.

7th Chords of the Harmonized Harmonic Minor Scale

Degree & Quality	Spelled from Key	Spelled from Its Own Root
i mi/maj7	1-♭3-5-7	1-♭3-5-7
ii mi7♭5	2-4-♭6-8	1-♭3-♭5-♭7
♭III maj7♯5	♭3-5-7-9	1-3-♯5-7
iv mi7	4-♭6-8-♭10	1-♭3-5-♭7
V7	5-7-9-11	1-3-5-♭7
♭vi maj7	♭6-8-♭10-12	1-3-5-7
vii dim7	7-9-11-♭13	1-♭3-♭5-♭♭7

In popular styles, the V7 chord associated with this scale is most commonly used, with the occasional i mi/maj7 and vii dim7. Usually a progression will revert back to chords derived from natural minor (i, ♭III, ♭VII) except on the V. We should however be familiar with the remaining chords and their arpeggios, as the uncommon may become common depending on the style of music.

Diatonic Seventh Arpeggios, A Harmonic Minor, Root Position
When playing the chords of the harmonized scale, it's necessary to move out of position to find playable voicings in the same inversion. Hearing these chords and their arpeggios one after another for eight measures may seem strange because normally only one or two at a time are used for temporary tension that is soon resolved. There are of course more possible fingerings for these chords and arpeggios, but this is a good starting place.

Track 6

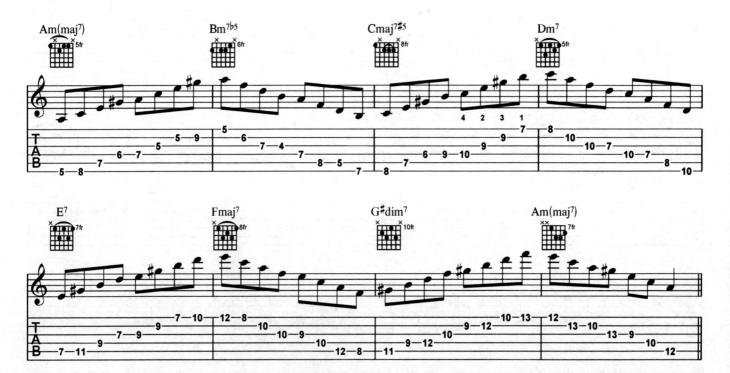

8

Unit 2: Phrygian Dominant

It may be easier to get the harmonic minor sound you want by only thinking of its 5th mode. This book assumes you understand modal relationships, but to put it briefly: D harmonic minor and A Phrygian Dominant, for example, share exactly the same set of fingerings. Pattern 2 of D harmonic minor is equivalent to Pattern 4 of A Phrygian Dominant.

For A Phrygian Dominant, we're starting from the 5th degree in D minor, even when no D minor chord appears. Now the root (1) of the pattern is A. The rest of the tones in the new scale count from there: B♭ is ♭2, C♯ is 3, etc. The augmented 2nd with its three-fret stretch in the pattern is now from ♭2 to 3.

A Phrygian Dominant

A	B♭	C♯	D	E	F	G	A
1	m2___M3		P4	P5	m6	m7	P8

Static Phrygian Dominant

In styles with Middle-Eastern influences (and some hard rock and metal), Phrygian Dominant may be used extensively without resolution, from the root of a major triad, dominant chord, power chord, or tonic note. Now it's a tense key center. This example uses E Phrygian Dominant, Pattern 4, equivalent to A harmonic minor, Pattern 2.

Track 7

Playing a major triad a half step above (or a minor seventh arpeggio a whole step below) the static tonal center makes interesting Phrygian Dominant sounds. This example uses B Phrygian Dominant, the 5th mode of E harmonic minor, so review that scale in 1st position, 4th position, and 6th position before you start.

(Note: in this book modal key signatures are avoided. Key signatures are either major or minor, or, when they wouldn't help, non-existent.)

Track 8

Emphasizing the diminished arpeggios that can be found within the scale is another common practice. This example uses D Phrygian Dominant (5th mode of G harmonic minor). Play the scale first to get the sound in your ears, then play the diminished seventh arpeggios starting from C, E♭, and F♯. The bassist would probably follow the written chord roots along with you.

Track 9

To develop chops in styles where the Phrygian Dominant mode persists for a long time, we can practice interval studies with it.

3rds in E Phrygian Dominant
Equal to A harmonic minor Pattern 5, this is E Phrygian Dominant Pattern 2.

Track 10

4ths in E Phrygian Dominant
This one is an octave higher, using Pattern 4. Notice that the diatonic 4th from 3-6 is diminished in quality, making it the same as a major 3rd, while the ones from 2 and 7 are augmented.

Track 11

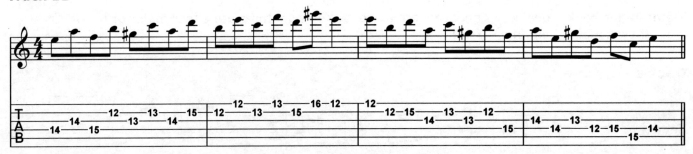

The 16-bar solo on the next page uses the D Phrygian Dominant scale (equivalent to G harmonic minor) almost exclusively. Starting in measure 9 a pattern of nine sixteenth notes is played five times, creating a polyrhythmic feel. There is a brief appearance of the C blues scale in measure 12. Alternating groups of 3 and 2 create more tension in measures 14 and 15 to set up the major-key release in the next section (not shown) of "Welcome Your Overlords".

Track 12

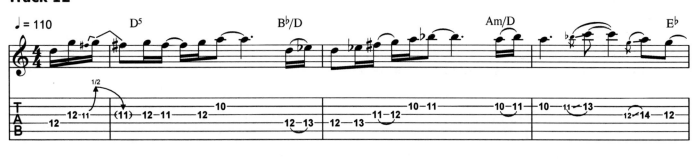

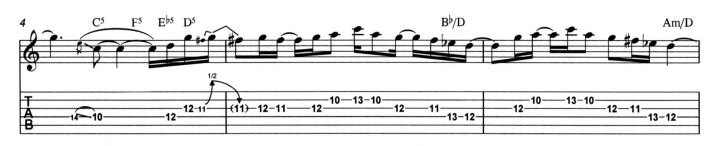

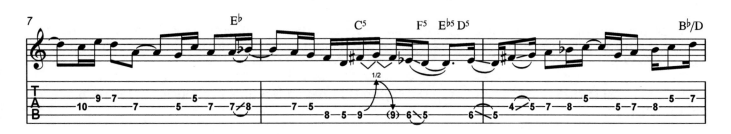

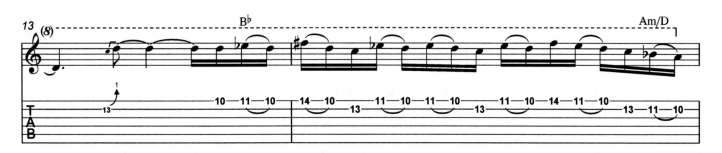

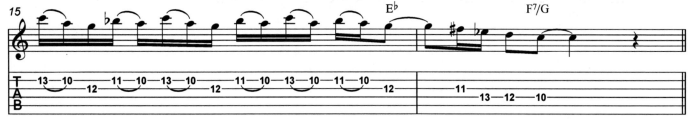

11

Other Harmonic Minor Modes

There is not always complete agreement about how the remaining modes of harmonic minor should be named. Here the same name as the major scale mode from the same starting note is used, with a reminder about the one degree that is different. The raised note is the root of mode 7; this mode gets a new name based on the closest melodic minor mode (Unit 6).

Mode	Chord
1. Harmonic Minor	m(maj7)
2. Locrian #6	m7♭5
3. Ionian #5 - Harmonic Major	maj7#5
4. Dorian #4	m7
5. Phrygian Dominant	7
6. Lydian #2	maj7
7. Superlocrian ♭♭7	dim7

You may find it sufficient to think only about the two modes of harmonic minor we've studied: harmonic minor from the root, and Phrygian Dominant. As with major and minor key centers, it's not completely necessary to think about a different mode for each chord when they end up being the same group of notes. Just be aware of how the notes relate to the chord of the moment.

For example, playing harmonic minor over a minor ii-V-i progression will automatically give you Locrian #6 over the diatonic iim7♭5 chord. The raised 7th of the related harmonic minor scale is the #6 degree over the iim7♭5.

In this progression that moves from Cm to D, playing D Phrygian Dominant produces C Dorian #4 over the Cm chord.

Track 13

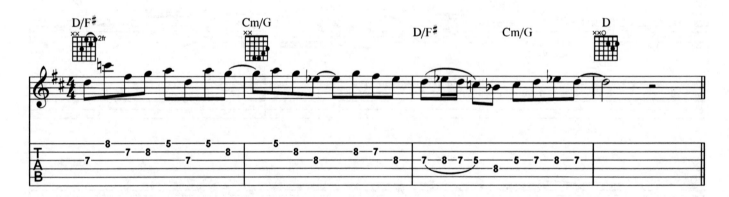

An exception to this is when you want to investigate new possibilities for existing harmonic situations. For example, you could introduce Dorian #4 over a minor chord, static or in a progression, where the related harmonic minor scale and its harmony have not previously been used.

In the case of harmonic minor and its modes, most "avoid" notes can be justified if you depart from Western classical tradition and treat chords as static drones over which melodic tension can resolve without a chord move.

Unit 3: Melodic Minor

This scale differs by one note from major, Dorian, or harmonic minor. With it comes a new set of modal applications. In its original classical form the scale reverts to natural minor when descending, but in modern and especially modal usage the notes are the same regardless of direction.

Melodic Minor Scale

1	M2	m3	P4	P5	M6	M7	P8

Here are five D melodic minor scale patterns.

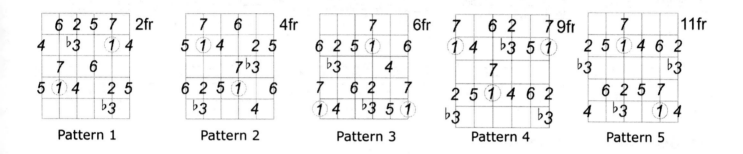

Pattern 1   Pattern 2   Pattern 3   Pattern 4   Pattern 5

You can play four notes on one string as shown using slides.

Track 14

Another option is to keep each degree on the same string it occupied in the comparable major scale pattern. This way there are never more than three notes per string and the pattern is more familiar. Here's D melodic minor with the 3rds on the same strings as in D major Pattern 1.

Getting the new shapes under your fingers (and into your ears) will take some time. Start with the goal of making patterns 2 and 4 of melodic minor usable on short notice. Take your time and practice in different keys.

Melodic Minor Lick

In measure 2 of this excerpt from "Healer," a blues and gospel-based ballad, Pattern 5 of A melodic minor is used when the IV chord in E switches from major (A/E) to minor (Am6). E major returns just before the next measure begins.

Track 15

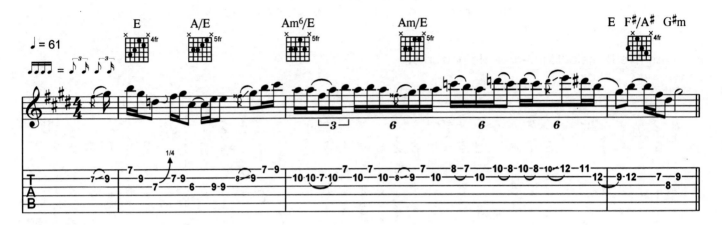

Melodic Minor Mode 1

Modern melodic minor reflects a minor chord with a major 7th, sometimes the result of a descending line, often in the bass. The minor chord may also contain a major 6 and/or 9. The melodic minor scale will sound good over a minor tonic triad where minor 6ths and 7ths are not present in any part. Once you are familiar with its sound, try it as a substitute for Dorian if you feel it fits the style of music.

Here G Dorian switches to G melodic minor and back as the descending line moves from root to major 7 to minor 7. Pluck the upper three strings of these chords with your fingers to avoid hitting the 5th string.

Track 16

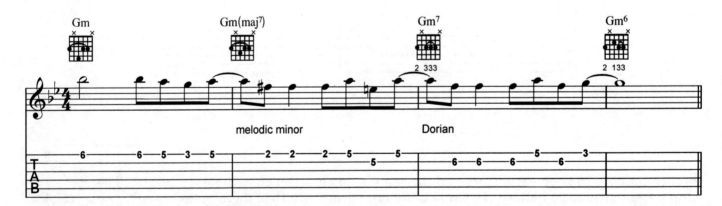

Modes of melodic minor are often used over short-lived non-diatonic chords in major or minor keys. As with harmonic minor it's often necessary to slip into (and out of) one of the melodic minor modes for a single measure or less. Learning to use this scale is harder than others, but the rewards of the effort are more movement and variation in the music.

The examples on this page (and those in later units) show how we need to be able to switch in and out of the melodic minor sound. It's important to realize this early. The interval studies that follow, however, stay inside the scale to help us familiarize ourselves with the scale as it might apply to a single chord.

14

Melodic Minor Interval Studies

Diatonic 3rds sound great right off the bat in this scale and will be especially useful if you're getting into jazz improvisation. These are in A melodic minor, Pattern 4.

Track 17

Alternating or "Square Wave" 3rds

This exercise is 1-3-4-2 in the four-note interval matrix. An ascending 3rd is followed by a step, then a descending 3rd. The latter half of this study makes a good lick for modes of melodic minor.

Track 18

4ths

As in harmonic minor, this sequence has a diminished 4th from 7 to ♭3. For the suggested rolling fingering, try pressing the ring finger down on top of the pinky.

Track 19

5ths in F Melodic Minor Pattern 2

Track 20

Scale Harmony

7th Chords of the Harmonized Melodic Minor Scale

Degree & Quality	Spelled from Key	Spelled from Its Own Root
i mi/maj7	1-♭3-5-7	1-♭3-5-7
ii mi7	2-4-6-8	1-♭3-5-♭7
♭III maj7♯5	♭3-5-7-9	1-3-♯5-7
iv dom7	4-6-8-♭10	1-3-5-♭7
V dom7	5-7-9-11	1-3-5-♭7
vi mi7♭5	6-8-♭10-12	1-♭3-♭5-♭7
vii mi7♭5	7-9-11-13	1-♭3-♭5-♭7

Here we arpeggiate the chords of the harmonized melodic minor scale without changing position. Start with Pattern 2 and add the other four patterns of this exercise as you progress. When playing the chords, move across positions to keep the same inversion.

Track 21

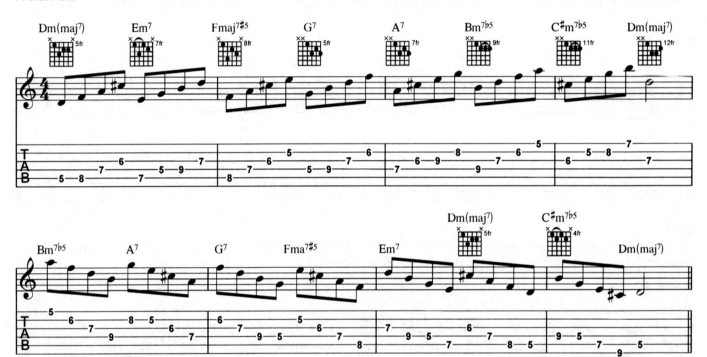

This table shows the most commonly-used (but maybe not the most logical) names for the modes of the melodic minor scale.

Mode	Chord	Degrees	Other Information
1. Melodic Minor	m(maj7)	1 2 ♭3 4 5 6 7	
2. Dorian ♭2	m7	1 ♭2 ♭3 4 5 6 ♭7	
3. Lydian ♯5	maj7♯5	1 2 3 ♯4 ♯5 6 7	
4. Lydian ♭7	7	1 2 3 ♯4 5 6 ♭7	a.k.a. Lydian Dominant
5. Mixolydian ♭6	7	1 2 3 4 5 ♭6 ♭7	
6. Locrian ♯2	m7♭5	1 2 ♭3 4 ♭5 ♭6 ♭7	the 2nd is actually major
7. Altered	m7♭5	1 ♭2 ♭3 ♭4 ♭5 ♭6 ♭7	= 1 ♭2 ♯2 3 ♭5 ♯5 ♭7

Although strict harmonization of the melodic minor scale produces a m7♭5 chord on the 7th degree, the 7th mode is used over dominant chords with altered 5ths and 9ths. The ♭4 is enharmonic with the major 3rd of a dominant chord. The ♭3 of the scale is enharmonic with the ♯9, a common altered extension.

Unit 4: Melodic Minor Mode 7 - The Altered Scale

The 7th mode of melodic minor is one of the most important and also one of the least difficult to start using. Another name for this scale is Superlocrian.

Altered Scale

1	m2	m3	d4	d5	m6	m7	P8

A *functioning* dominant chord is one that resolves, usually up a fourth from V7-I or V7-i. In a major key (V7-I) we continue to play the major scale over the functioning V7 chord, producing Mixolydian. In a minor key (V7-i) we've used the harmonic minor scale of the i over a functioning V7. The introduction of the leading tone increases the tension on the V chord.

The altered scale is another useful choice to play over a functioning V chord in a minor key, partly because it further increases tension by completely avoiding the tonic note until the i chord arrives. Notice how this line circles chromatically around the A note before landing on it. The E altered scale is equal to F melodic minor.

Track 22

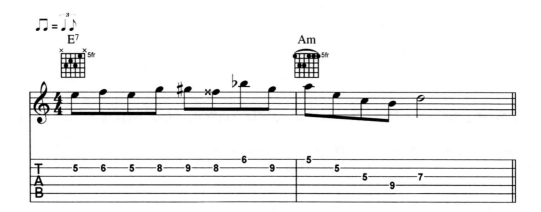

The altered scale is equivalent to the notes of a melodic minor scale a half-step above the root of a dominant chord. Besides the tones that cannot change if you want a dominant chord (root, 3rd, and ♭7—also called the *shell* of the chord), it includes all possible altered chord tones and extensions (♭5 ♯5 ♭9 ♯9).

Track 23

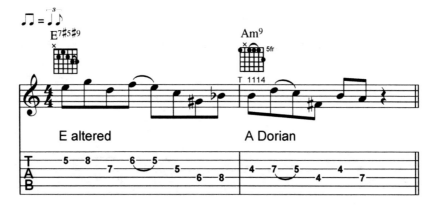

Just moving up a fret from a dominant chord and playing any note of a melodic minor scale, however, while a quick way to find it, might not convince you that this is a sound you want to use. It is best to think of the relationship between the scale and the chord it is played over, and how it resolves into the chord that normally follows.

If unaltered notes 5, 9, 11, or 13 (6) are present in the chord, the tones of the altered scale may clash to a degree that goes beyond tension and becomes noise. Try it, but consider the rhythmic placement of the tension.

You can almost always use the altered scale over a V7 chord that has the usual extensions in a minor key, style permitting. If that V chord has a ♭5, #5, ♭9, #9, or some combination of these, it's the most inside choice.

Making It Easier
To get started with the altered sound try playing a chord tone, then grabbing a mi/maj9 arpeggio up a half step from the root of the dominant chord. Note, however, that this does not include the most challenging note of the scale, in this case D♭.

Track 24

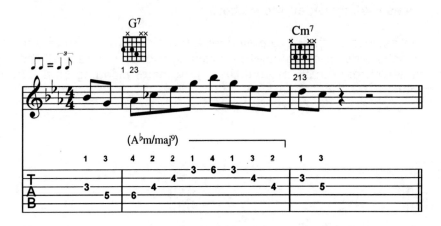

Altered on Secondary Dominants with Intended Minor Targets

The altered scale is a good alternative to Phrygian Dominant on a secondary dominant whose intended resolution is a diatonic minor chord. In a major key the minor triads are ii, iii, and vi. Their respective dominants are
- "five of two": V7/ii (VI7 - "six dominant")
- "five of three": V7/iii (VIII7 - "seven dominant")
- "five of six": V7/vi (III7 - "three dominant").

The names in parentheses are often used when describing progressions to other musicians. They're easier because they don't bother naming the intended target, which may or may not come after the chord being described. Let's check out these secondary dominants in the key of C major. For each altered scale choice, try Phrygian Dominant in the same place. Use shell voicings (R-3-♭7 only) for the dominant chords.

V7/ii (VI7)
First we've got the V7/ii, A7 here, and the A altered scale is equal to B♭ melodic minor.

Track 25

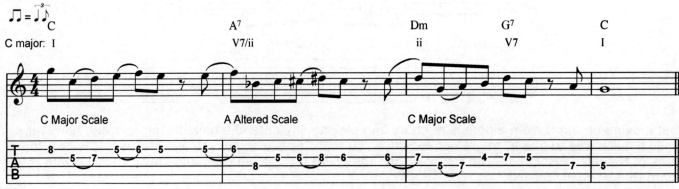

V7/iii (VIII7)

The B altered scale is the same as C melodic minor, so all the notes are the same as the major key center except one (E♭), which is not played in this example.

Track 26

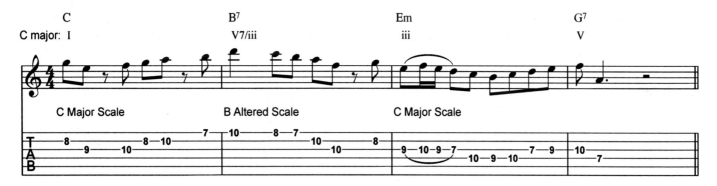

V7/vi (III7)

The remaining secondary dominant with an intended minor resolution is the V7/vi or III7.

Track 27

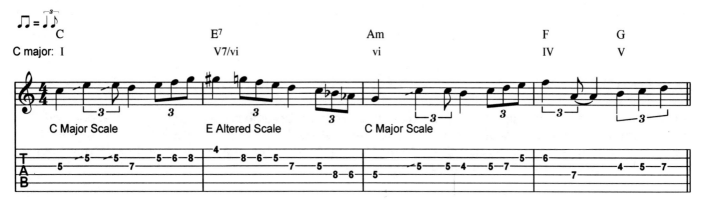

V7/v (II7) in Minor

The v chord in a minor key is diatonically minor (although it is frequently converted to dominant, as we saw in the harmonic minor unit). Again, we can increase movement toward this chord by altering its respective V. The deciding factor in using the altered scale is the intended or actual root movement—and of course, your ear.

In measure 3 of this excerpt from "Mojito" there's a complete B altered scale over V/v (II7) in the key of Am (only the chord root, B, is omitted from the line). The pickup and measure 1 have an interesting chromatic lick over a functioning V/iv (I7). Measure 2 has a chromatic lower neighbor tone.

Track 28

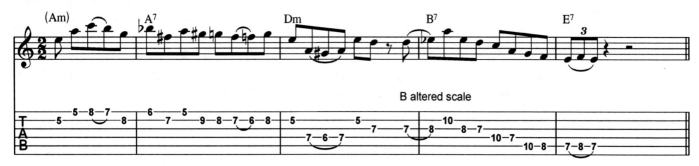

Secondary Dominants with Intended Major Targets

It's more challenging to the ear, but secondary dominants that resolve to chords based on major triads (V⁷/IV, V⁷/V) may also take some alterations.

V7/IV (I7)

For the first situation, try altering the I⁷ chord in a jazzy uptempo blues just before moving to the IV. In roots styles you may not like the altered sound on the I. As shown in measures 3 and 4 relate scales to the overall key center when possible for smooth melodic construction, but also be aware of their relation to the bar harmony.

Track 29

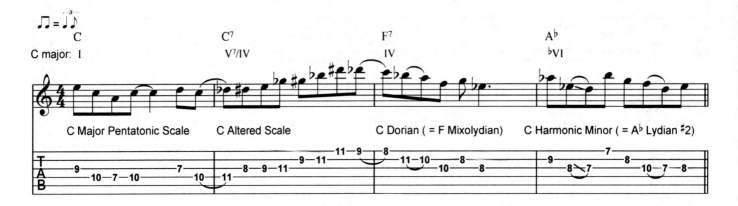

V7/V (II7)

The V⁷/V usually does not take the altered scale but can sometimes have a ♭9 that is best expressed by the dominant diminished scale, which we'll see later. If the V⁷/V has no alterations like this typical example, then you'll play Mixolydian. If there are non-diatonic notes in any chord, follow them if your line should cross that area. Here it happens in measure 4.

Track 30

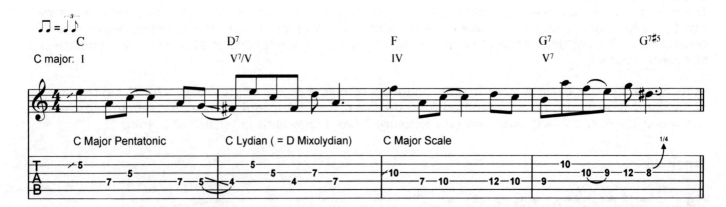

The jazz standard "Stella by Starlight" is good for working on altered scale applications. It has dominant chords that may be altered with intended resolutions to ii, iii, vi, and the I chord in major.

Unit 5: Melodic Minor Mode 4 - Lydian ♭7

Over non-diatonic dominant chords, we decide between several possible scale choices, based on chord extensions if they exist, or by examining the surrounding chords.

Functioning Dominants and Key Changes

First we'll look at the case where a new scale type is not needed. If a ♭II, ♭III, ♭V, ♭VI, or ♭VII functions as a V to a major or minor chord that follows it, you can consider it a temporary key change as if you'd found a ii-V in traditional harmony. Listen closely to be sure the scale conforms to what you hear the chords doing. Here you can modulate to the key of D♭ major, which gives A♭ Mixolydian on the A♭7. Switch back to C major when that key resumes.

Track 31

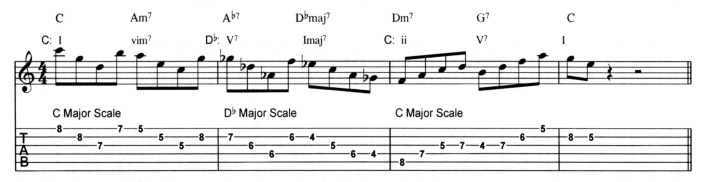

The 4th degree in the Mixolydian and Phrygian Dominant modes is the tonic of the parent major or minor scale, respectively. If for example you're playing over a G7 chord, its 4th is C, and C or Cm is the chord to which you'd expect to resolve.

Non-Functioning Dominants

Compared to that perfect 4th, using the ♯11 (the same as ♯4 or ♭5) **removes the expectation** that the next chord will be a 4th higher, making it appropriate on non-diatonic dominant 7th chords that have no diatonic target and do not resolve. The ♭5 or ♯11 keeps the chord from pushing you into a different key or toward another chord. Instead of tensely pointing at a destination, it floats neutrally until functional harmony resumes. Here are some stock voicings of dominant chords with ♭5 or ♯11.

The Lydian ♭7 scale (4th mode of melodic minor, also called Lydian Dominant) resembles Mixolydian but has a ♯4, and fits the dominant 7♯11 or 7♭5 chord. Though it's important to know it is the fourth mode of melodic minor, you should eventually learn its patterns from their roots.

Lydian ♭7

| 1 | M2 | M3 | a4 | P5 | M6 | m7 | P8 |

When a dominant chord with this single alteration (♯4/♯11 or ♭5) appears, Lydian Dominant is usually the correct scale to fit it. More importantly, if a non-diatonic triad or dominant chord would have a ♯11 if it were extended using notes from the key, then Lydian Dominant would again be the right choice.

This sound occurs frequently in popular music, sometimes just as a non-diatonic triad or bass note beneath one or two melody notes, making it hard to know which scales would best fit. The examples in this unit have a high density of notes to give you a chance to hear and practice the new sound more. In melodic improvisation it will often be best to play fewer notes.

> Depending on the style of music, Lydian Dominant might sound too jazzy for the song, even when it is more technically "inside" than Mixolydian.

Non-Functioning Dominants in Major Keys

New (for us) non-functioning dominant chords where Lydian ♭7 is called for can occur in major keys on the non-diatonic starting notes ♭II, ♭III, ♭V, ♭VI, and ♭VII. These examples are all in one key (C) to make things easier to understand. The theory is the same in all the other major keys and each needs to be practiced on the guitar.

Play each of the following chord progressions several times before working on the single-note line.

♭II
The first example has the ♭II (D♭7) at the end. Because the example repeats, we see this chord is not starting a key change to G♭, so we can play Lydian Dominant.

Track 32

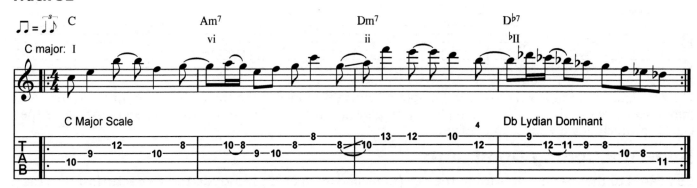

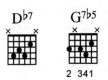

The ♭II, ♭III, ♭V, ♭VI, and ♭VII are also *tritone substitutes* for dominant 7♭5 chords a tritone (three whole steps) above or below. The 3rd and 7th of each are enharmonic to the 7th and 3rd of the interchangeable substitute chord. Often a "flat-five sub" like this is used to create a chromatic bass line.

♭III
If the ♭III7 were a functioning dominant chord it would resolve to ♭VI. This ostensible target is non-diatonic in a major key, so we can play Lydian Dominant instead of Mixolydian.

Track 33

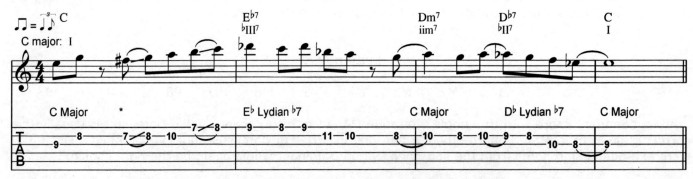

*Another chromatic neighbor tone: a note on the upbeat that leads into an on-beat chord tone.

♭VI

If a ♭VI were functioning, it would resolve to ♭II. There is no ♭II in a major key, so this is another place we can play Lydian Dominant.

Track 34

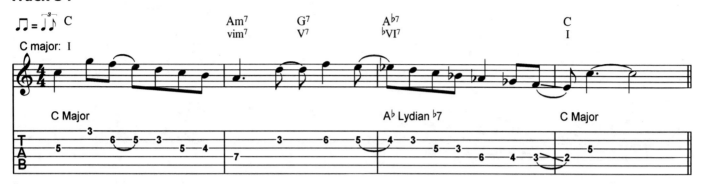

♭V

In a blues-based situation you can try floating over the "outside" chord with the blues scale from the key center, or pick a few nice notes that are common to it and Lydian ♭7 of the non-diatonic dominant.

Track 35

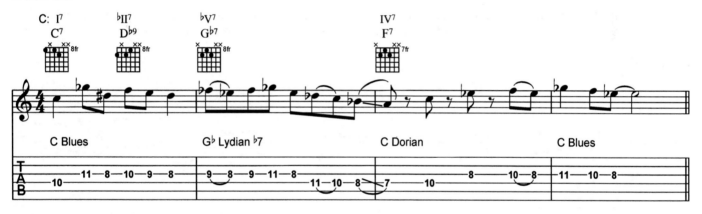

♭VII

As well as modal interchange (yet to be covered), ♭VII⁷ may be considered as a non-functioning dominant with the same result.

Track 36

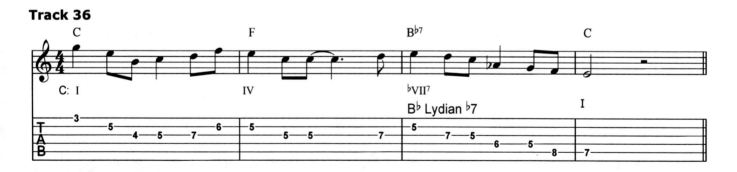

On the next page an excerpt in D from "Teabag" uses C Lydian ♭7 over the ♭VII⁷ and doesn't bother to switch on the I chord (measure 2). The result over that chord is D Mixolydian ♭6, which we'll see again in the next unit.

23

Non-Functioning Dominants in Minor Keys

♭VI

A♭7 (replacing the diatonic A♭maj7) in C minor would resolve to D♭ if it were functioning, but there's no D♭ in the key of Cm. We can play A♭ Lydian ♭7. The C blues scale would also sound good here.

Track 38

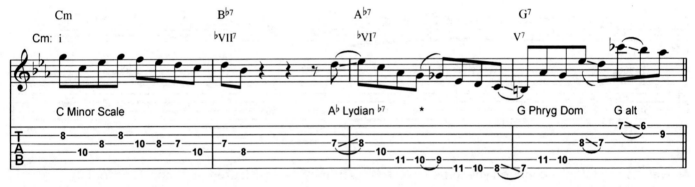

*passing tone between chord factors 1 and ♭7.

♭II

D♭7, the ♭II7 here, would resolve to G♭ if it were functioning. There is no G♭ in Cm, so we can play D♭ Lydian ♭7. D♭7 is also a tritone substitute for G7, the functioning V chord. The same scale applies.

Track 39

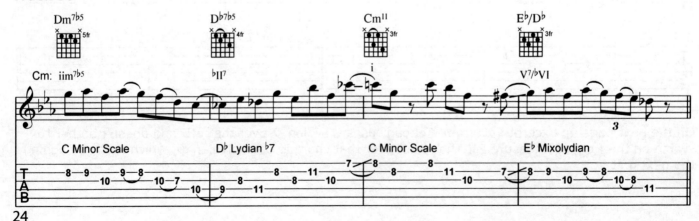

Unit 6: More Melodic Minor Modes

These modes of melodic minor don't have any special considerations like dominant functionality. They're often just matched to tones or extensions found in a non-diatonic one- or two-chord move.

Mode 6: Locrian #2

Lesser in importance but still used, the 6th mode of melodic minor is Locrian #2. The second degree of the scale is actually major, making it only sharp in comparison with the ♭2 found in Locrian, the seventh major scale mode.

Locrian #2

1	M2	m3	P4	d5	m6	m7	P8

Locrian #2 specifically fits a m9♭5 chord.

Dm9♭5

Locrian #2 is an alternative to Locrian over the m7♭5 chord in a minor ii-V-i. The 2nd degree of the scale is the major 3rd of the key center so it may create an expectation that you will resolve to a major I chord.

Track 40

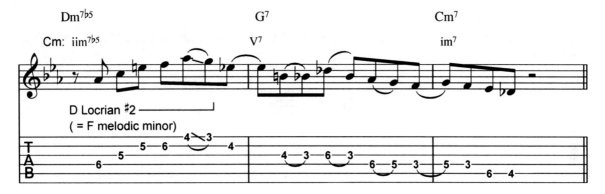

Mode 3: Lydian #5

Lydian #5

1	M2	M3	a4	a5	M6	M7	P8

This mode specifically fits a maj7#5 chord.

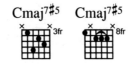

Cmaj7#5   Cmaj7#5

You can use Lydian #5 instead of Lydian over a maj7 chord built on a non-diatonic root in a major key. It will help if your accompanist leaves out the 5th (or alters it).

Track 41

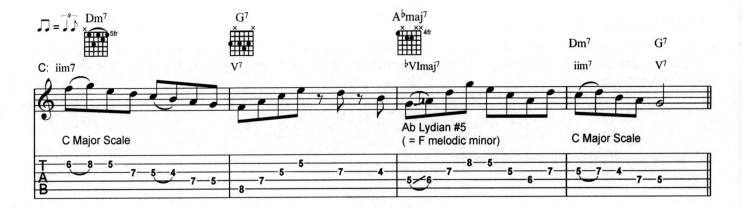

Mode 5: Mixolydian ♭6

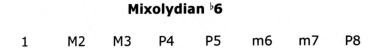

Mixolydian ♭6

| 1 | M2 | M3 | P4 | P5 | m6 | m7 | P8 |

This mode fits a dominant chord with a #5 or ♭13 altered extension only, and specifically one that includes a natural 9th.

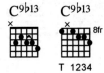

This example has Mixolydian ♭6 applied to the V chord in a turnaround for a blues ballad.

Track 42

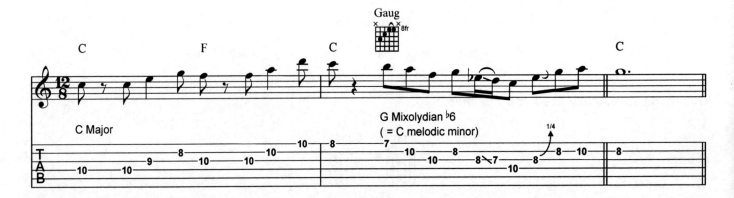

26

Unit 7: Melodic Minor for Modal Interchange

One type of *modal interchange* is—when in a major key—chords are borrowed from the minor key starting from the same tonic (the *parallel* minor). Melodic minor modes can fit some instances of this as an alternative to the natural minor scale, especially when the major 3rd of the key shows up in the interchange chord.

In all the following cases you'd use the melodic minor scale up a fourth from the tonic chord. You can think of this as a switch from major to Mixolydian ♭6 over the key center compared to the usual parallel switch from major to minor. Switching to natural minor gives you the ♭3, ♭6, and ♭7 of the key center; switching to Mixolydian ♭6 keeps the major 3rd, only changing the 6th and 7th.

These harmonic situations are shown in rough order of frequency of occurrence and difficulty of application. Transpose these to different major keys, and find more voicings for the chords if your fretboard knowledge allows it.

ivm
First, we can borrow a minor iv chord—Fm (or Fm/maj7 or Fm6)—from the key of C minor, and play F melodic minor over it.

Track 43

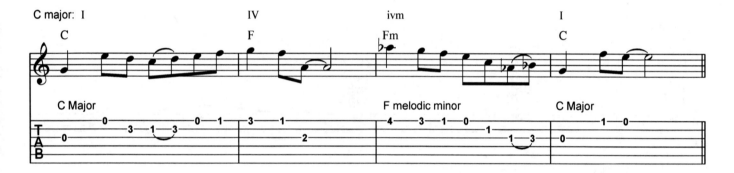

Though often associated with melancholy in pop songs (e.g., Radiohead's "Creep"), the ♭6 tone can be introduced for less-pronounced effects. In this excerpt from "Off the Lip" it's in a rock context where the IV is just a power chord, allowing it to be interpreted as either major or minor, or both in succession (meas. 2, 3).

Track 44

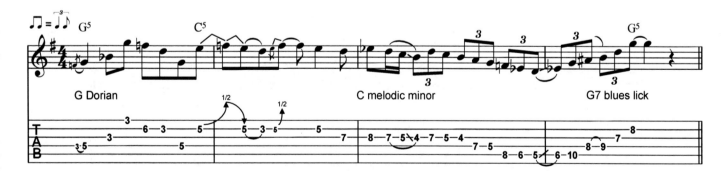

27

♭VII

If we borrow B♭7, for a ♭VII in the key of C major, playing F melodic minor over it gives us Lydian ♭7. This sound is used on the outro of Derek and the Dominos' original recording of "Layla," at 3:28.

Track 45

iim7♭5

If instead of Dm7 for the ii chord we borrow Dm7♭5 from the parallel key of C minor, we can play F melodic minor to get D Locrian #2. Notice the chromatic line created by the top notes of the chords in this example.

Track 46

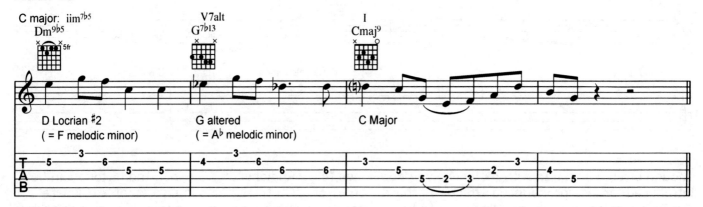

Vsus4♭9

Here a Vsus4♭9 is presented in its simplest case as a V-I move for a pop song.

Track 47

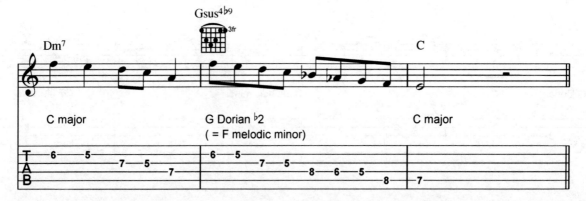

The sus4♭9 chord can also be used as an interesting static tonal center. In that context it may feel more complex, so you might just let the chord ring without a lot of melodic activity so the listener can digest it. For the static situation, Phrygian or Phrygian Dominant are better options.

Unit 8: The Diminished Scale

The two diminished scales are symmetrical, consisting of a repeating pattern of either 1) a whole and then a half step ("whole-half"), or 2) a half and then a whole step ("half-whole"). When the word "diminished" is used by itself regarding a scale, you can assume it means the whole-half scale, which fits a diminished 7th chord.

The diminished scale has 8 tones within the octave, so one scale degree number must be repeated with a different accidental. In writing you may see, for example, two pitches labeled as the 7th; one diminished, one major.

Diminished Whole-Half Scale

1	M2	m3	P4	d5	m6	d7	M7	P8

Diminished (Whole-Half) Scale Patterns

From 6th-string Root

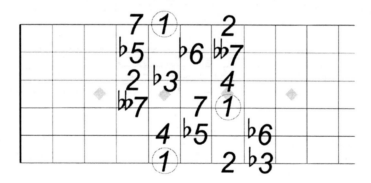

From 5th-string Root

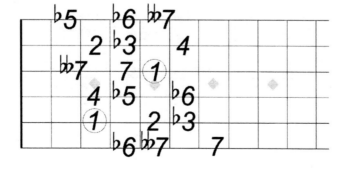

29

The symmetry of the diminished scale makes it so that all its positional three-note-per-string patterns could look one of the above two ways. Only the scale degree numbers would change as you move through positions using the same fingering shapes. For example, the first pattern could be moved to fret 2 to start with G♭, the ♭♭7 degree of A.

Many players prefer to find and play just the first pattern when a diminished scale is needed. It repeats at three-fret intervals so it's never far from your current position. Identical fingering starting from C at fret 8 gives you the same scale; likewise from E♭ at fret 11 and F♯ at fret 14.

When you need any diminished scale the first and main job is to figure out where to play the pattern. That's hard enough, as you'll see when you try to start in the middle of it. If you've found A diminished, you're also playing the right pattern for C, E♭/D♯, and F♯/G♭. Even before this skill is reliable you should work at knowing the notes in relation to the chord and key of the moment. This will be musically significant. The fact that the fingering repeats does not mean all the notes sound the same in relation to the key center they are played over.

A traditional use of a diminished 7th chord is to pass between diatonic chords a whole step apart, for example when descending from iii to ii. The 7th of the key is the ♭6 over the diminished chord here, a common melodic choice for composers.

Track 48

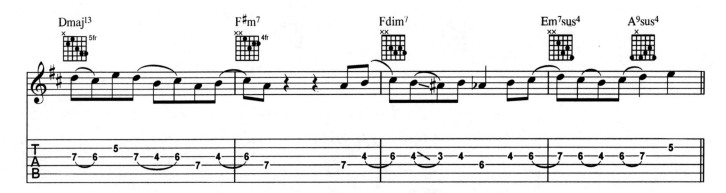

Since the diminished scale pattern repeats at three-fret intervals, any diminished scale must be equal to C, C♯, or D diminished. This means there is (only) one chance in three that a random starting place will yield the correct scale for a given diminished chord.

Guitarists use symmetry in various ways to help find the notes of the scale and move around in it. One possible way is to consider that the scale is comprised of two minor *tetrachords* (four-note scale fragments) a tritone apart.

A six-note fingering shape (134 124) repeats on three stringsets, with a shift for the bottom two strings.

A handy way to break out of playing successive scale steps on the top four strings is to recognize that any 3-note shape is repeated when you skip a string.

Track 49

The shapes repeat the same way on the bottom strings with a one-fret shift.

Track 50

A repeating four-note-per-string pattern (half-whole-half) on every string slides up or down the fretboard.

Diminished 7th arpeggios consist of consecutive minor 3rds only.

Within the A diminished scale the same arpeggio resides a half-step below the one(s) just mentioned. This means there are also B diminished, D diminished, and F diminished arpeggios within the scale.

You can quickly get a cool diminished lick by playing each diminished triad starting from a tone of a diminished chord, then another one a half step below (or a whole step above).

Track 51

Diminished Sequences and Interval Studies

The diminished scale carries some ambiguity with it, since every other of its notes could be its root and the chord it is played over (or implies) may be followed by almost any other. Repetitive phrases and shapes give the listener a chance to recognize a pattern and experience a sense of familiarity. You can also create patterns of accents with your articulations: hammer-ons, pulloffs, slides, bends, picking directions, etc.

Let's start with an easy group-of-four scale sequence.

Track 52

Now reverse the groups of four.

Track 53

3rds
All 3rds diatonic to the scale are minor. Any major 3rds in the scale are technically diminished 4ths.

Track 54

Square Wave 3rds
Now alternate ascending and descending 3rds: 1342.

Track 55

More Four-Note Sequences
Try 3124:

Track 56

and 3142.

Track 57

4ths

There are alternating perfect and diminished 4ths.

Track 58

"Coltrane" Pattern

This diminished sequence uses square wave fourths: up one, down the next. Start again down a ♭3.

Track 59

When you start to hear the above melodic contour, play it in the positional fingering pattern.

Track 60

5ths

The diatonic 5ths starting from the root are all diminished.

Track 61

6ths

Alternating minor and diminished 6ths (enharmonic with perfect 5ths) produce some B-movie-style tension.

Track 62

Two Kinds of 7ths

The diminished 7ths are enharmonic with major 6ths, moving up in alternating whole and half steps. Learn this example well to prepare for some interesting outside jazz and blues sounds we'll see in the next unit. Ascend and descend, and slide between alternating intervals.

Track 63

There are also alternating major and minor 7ths in the scale.

Track 64

Unit 9: The Dominant Diminished Scale

The two diminished scales share the same fingerings, so we can apply the pattern we already know just by starting a half-step above a dominant 7th chord. The four previous pages of intervallic ideas would apply to A♭7, B7, D7, and F7.

Dominant Diminished or Diminished Half, Whole

1	m2	a2	M3	d5	a5	M6	m7	P8

As with the diminished scale, steps of the dominant diminished scale could be named a number of different ways. They are named here in relation to a dominant chord.

Review unaltered dominant 7th chords and arpeggios in all five fingering patterns. Patterns 2 and 4 at the least should be solidly under your fingers before you apply dominant diminished. They're shown here with their stock dominant chord voicings; all are D7 chords when played at the positions marked.

   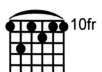 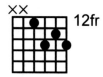

Now find the chord roots and place the arpeggios with their circled roots in the same position. Start with a Pattern 1 D7 arpeggio with roots on frets 3 and 5.

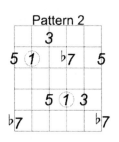 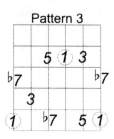 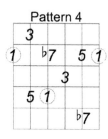

After playing all the patterns in D to cover the fretboard, switch to G and start over with Pattern 4 in 2nd position, then start over in C with Pattern 2 in 2nd position, then find and play them in F, B♭, and E♭.

A Half Step *above* the Root

Now let's focus on Pattern 4 of C7. The same principles will apply to all five. To the existing shape we'll first add the ♭9 in every register (D♭), a half step above the root. Sometimes this one extra note will be all you want, and you may only want it in the higher register. Instead of throwing in all the notes of dominant diminished at once, start by adding this one.

Track 65

37

Now we have a C7♭9 arpeggio (and chord). If the C were omitted, we'd have a D♭dim7 (or C#dim7). The 3, 5, and ♭7 of the dominant chord are the ♭3, ♭5, and ♭♭7 of the diminished chord a half step higher.

Go through as many of the other four dominant arpeggio shapes as you already know and add ♭9s in every octave. If you need to review the basic dominant shapes, add them to your practice schedule as an item separate from dominant diminished. If you want to proceed with this unit at the same time, go slowly, knowing that any missing prerequisites will make it harder.

Half Steps *below* the Other Tones

So far you have added a tone (♭9) a half step **above** the roots of the dominant arpeggio. Now next to each remaining tone (3-5-♭7), add a half step **below** (#9, ♭5, and 13). In this diagram the added notes are black dots next to the chord tones in a Pattern 4 dominant 7th arpeggio.

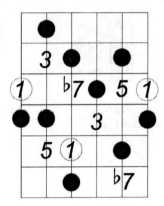

Track 66

When applying this sound on a dominant chord, add one or more of the new notes to get a taste of the dom-dim sound. Adding all of them will give you the complete scale, but keep the original 7th arpeggio shape in mind. If you think of it this way you a) will be emphasizing the chord tones first and adding the others in relation to them, b) won't have to think about the diminished scale patterns much, and c) will get a smoother, more musical sound.

This means that sometimes you'll play four notes on some strings and only two on others, but that's completely fine if it assists you in your phrasing. You'll also do more position shifting in the middle of phrases when using this sound.

When you're ready, add the chromatic notes below 3, 5, and ♭7 in every octave of the other four dominant arpeggio shapes on page 37.

Relating Dominant and Diminished Chords

Check out how the same diminished chord shapes always result from raising the root of a dominant 7th chord. For each stringset shown there are four inversions.

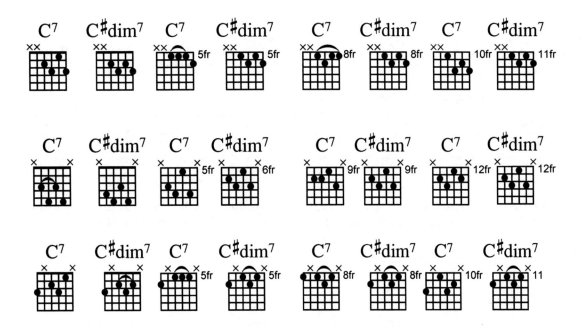

A diminished 7th chord can function as a 7♭9 chord a half step below any of its tones. Any of the above diminished chords could equal C7♭9, E♭7♭9, F♯7♭9, or A7♭9. There are two scale possibilities for the diminished chord, depending on the surrounding chords.

> Some improvisors disregard the second consideration below and use the diminished scale or arpeggio for every diminished chord, regardless of the surrounding chords.

1: The dim7 Chord as 13♭9: The "Dominant Diminished Chord"

In most cases the diminished (whole, half) scale is the best choice for the **diminished** chord.

Over the related dominant chords as shown above this equals the dominant diminished (half, whole) scale: a combination of unaltered and altered tones (3, 5, ♭7, and ♭9 from the diminished chord, and then 13, ♯9, and ♯4/♭5 from the scale.)

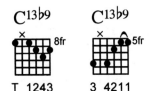

When a 7♭9 chord does **not** have a minor chord a 4th higher as its intended target (discussed next), it can be extended to dominant 13♭9. In this C13♭9 chord, the 13th is A. The dominant diminished scale is the only one we've learned that fits this chord.

You can use dominant diminished not just to fit this new chord but to create tension over a 4-note dominant chord, major triad, or even a bass note.

With the ♭9 and 6th (equivalent to the 13th) you get an A major triad (and A7) over C7. Following the symmetry, the complete scale contains A7, F♯7, and E♭7.

Here C7 is functioning as the V chord in the key of F. Major triads a minor 3rd apart are derived from the C dominant diminished scale.

Track 67

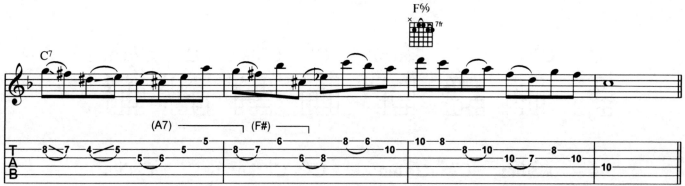

Dominant diminished is especially good on the V7/V, a secondary dominant with a major intended target. In measure 3 here we have dominant diminished on the V7/V in the key of G.

Track 68

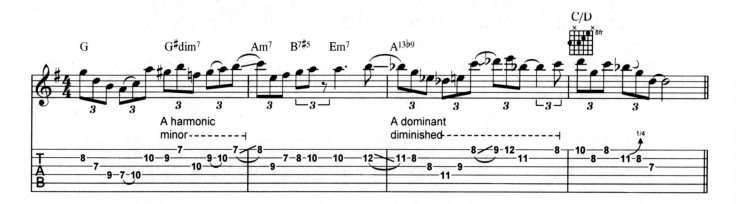

2: The dim7 Chord as a Functioning Dominant with Minor Target

Since the dim7 chord is the vii in a harmonized harmonic minor scale (Unit 1), the related harmonic minor scale will work over a functioning diminished 7th chord with a minor target. For each functioning V chord in Unit 1 (E7 on Tracks 1-4) you could substitute G#dim7 or any of its equivalents: Bdim7, Ddim7 or Fdim7.

When we compared the altered scale to harmonic minor in Unit 4 we saw each of the three secondary dominants with intended minor targets: V/ii, V/iii, V/vi. Now that same dominant tension is being expressed by a diminished chord a half step higher (or any of its equivalents). For any of those examples, we could go back and substitute a viidim7 chord for the V7 shell voicing (1-3-♭7). Now the altered scale would clash with the chord, so we'd use the harmonic minor of the intended target (or as noted in the earlier gray box we can try the diminished scale).

Take another look at Track 68 on this page. The diminished chord in measure 1 contains the leading tone of the minor chord that follows (for A minor, the leading tone is G#), so it is functioning as its V7. In this case you can play A harmonic minor on the G#dim7 because it is an inversion of E7♭9. Revert to G major when the Am chord arrives, because it is the diatonic ii chord in that key.

40

Dominant Diminished on the Blues

The I7 and V7 chords in a blues are functioning dominants with major targets, so we can play dominant diminished from the roots of each of them. I7 is a secondary dominant: the V/IV, and V7 is the dominant chord in the key; it resolves to I.

Further, the IV7 chord in measure 5 of a twelve-bar blues progression is often followed by a diminished chord a half step higher. You can hear that the same diminished scale works over both IV and #ivdim7 chords. The conclusion, on paper at least, is that you can play dominant diminished on each of the three main chords in the blues.

Here's a 12-bar blues in B♭ used at MI to supplement the Blues Level II class, where we start incorporating some jazz ideas. It includes obvious phrases in dominant diminished and the altered scale, and a blues scale phrase near the end. The I chord (B♭7) should have its 5th omitted or altered if you use the altered scale. The dominant diminished lines track the chord tones closely as described at the beginning of this unit.

Track 69

As If That Weren't Enough

From the roots of the four dominant chords related by diminished harmony there are major, minor, and diminished triads, and dominant 7, major 6, minor 6, minor 7, m7♭5, and dim7 four-note chords and arpeggios. All may be found minor 3rds apart and may be arpeggiated in any inversion to give structure to a dominant diminished line.

There are so many possibilities that you can easily get lost trying to decide which to use and end up playing nothing over this normally short-lived sound. Find one or two simple ideas that work for you. Again, the dominant arpeggio with chromatic neighbor tones is a good starting point.

The next example is a descending dominant arpeggio followed by a diminished shape from one of its higher extensions. The sequence is eight notes long.

Track 70

Here's one way to take the sequence up in minor 3rds without too much shifting.

Track 71

Given a long enough time on one chord (or multiple chords of similar quality a minor 3rd apart), you can use the sequence to develop a lick. This one is an excerpt from "In the Fine Texas Tradition."

Track 72

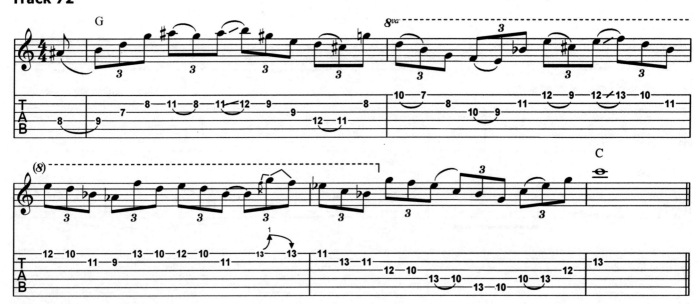

Notice that the diminished (whole, half) scale is pretty close to blues and Dorian modes, with its minor 3rd, ♭5, and major 6th. Try using it to spice up rockabilly and blues-rock licks.

Track 73

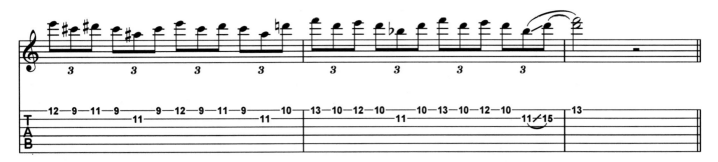

Here's one more excerpt, this time from "Devil's House Party." At the end of measure 3 there are parallel shapes on frets 7 and 9 of strings 1 and 3.

Track 74

With practice and experimentation you can learn to use dominant diminished to create controlled tension on nearly any chord that is based on a major triad. Likewise, you can force diminished (whole, half) over most chords based on minor or diminished triads. With that in mind, remember that music should have a balance of tension and resolution, and the listener feels a payoff when the resolution is right.

Conclusion

Sounds derived from the three scale sources in this book may feel awkward at first, and won't work in every song. Try to hear them first in terms of jazz, blues, ragtime, or gospel, as these styles still have the influence of classic functional harmony.

Conversely, realize that the book is only meant to broaden and not limit your possibilities. There are many options that we did not cover. If your ear tells you a different scale or chord works in a given situation, by all means—play it!

This book is a result of years (over 25 now—it's hard to believe!) in the rooms at Musicians Institute, jamming with students and other instructors. I'd like to thank them all for teaching me and for letting me join in their explorations.

Lightning Source UK Ltd.
Milton Keynes UK
UKOW02f0119130314

228068UK00014B/557/P